CLASS 66

CLASS 66

Fred Kerr

Pen & Sword
TRANSPORT

First published in Great Britain in 2020 by
Pen & Sword Transport
An imprint of
Pen & Sword Books Ltd
47 Church Street
Barnsley
South Yorkshire
S70 2AS

Copyright © Fred Kerr 2020

ISBN 978 1 52677 625 9

The right of Fred Kerr to be identified as Author of this work has
been asserted by him in accordance with the Copyright, Designs and Patents
Act 1988.

A CIP catalogue record for this book is
available from the British Library.

All rights reserved. No part of this book may be reproduced or transmitted
in any form or by any means, electronic or mechanical including photocopying,
recording or by any information storage and retrieval system, without
permission from the Publisher in writing.

Typeset in 11pt Minion by Mac Style
Printed and bound by Printworks Global Ltd, London/Hong Kong

Pen & Sword Books Limited incorporates the imprints of Atlas, Archaeology, Aviation, Discovery, Family History, Fiction, History, Maritime, Military, Military Classics, Politics, Select, Transport, True Crime, Air World, Frontline Publishing, Leo Cooper, Remember When, Seaforth Publishing, The Praetorian Press, Wharncliffe Local History, Wharncliffe Transport, Wharncliffe True Crime and White Owl.

For a complete list of Pen & Sword titles please contact
PEN & SWORD BOOKS LIMITED
47 Church Street, Barnsley, South Yorkshire, S70 2AS, England
E-mail: enquiries@pen-and-sword.co.uk
Website: www.pen-and-sword.co.uk

Front Cover: GBRf Class 66/7 66703 *Doncaster PSB 1981–2002* eases through Doncaster on 19 January 2012 while working an Immingham–Eggborough Power Station coal service.
Rear Cover: EWSR Class 66/0 66186 stables in Aberdeen Guild St on 7 March 2004 prior to continuing to Laurencekirk the following day.

Contents

Introduction 6

Section 1: Locomotive Operations 7
1.1: Locomotive Operators 7
1.2: Locomotive Deliveries 9
1.3: Customer Liveries 11
1.4: Operating Regions 11

Section 2: UK Regions 12
2.1: Eastern Region South 12
2.2: Yorkshire & Lincolnshire 22
2.3: Northern England 38
2.4: LM Region South 65
2.5: LM Region North West 78
2.6: Wales and Borders 107
2.7: Thames and Cotswolds 112
2.8: Wessex and West Country 119
2.9: South and South East 129
2.10: Scotland 139

Section 3: Finale 159

Introduction

The Class 66 design emanated from an order placed by the English Welsh Scottish Railways (EWSR) in May 1996 following its purchase of the UK Freight Operating companies when British Railways (BR) was privatised on 1 April 1994. The new company's early decision to undertake a locomotive fleet review in May 1996, comprising Classes 20, 31, 33, 47, 56, 58, 73 and 86, identified that the repair costs were greater than the replacement cost for many locomotives, hence an order was placed with the American firm of General Motors (GM) for 250 locomotives.

The design of the new order was based on BR's Class 59 which had been supplied by GM to the firms of Foster Yeoman and Associated Roadstone Corporation (ARC) in 1985 and 1989 respectively from its La Grange factory in Illinois. The new order differed by being built in the company's factory at London, Ontario, and fitted with a more recent drive chain including the 12-cylinder 2-stroke 12N-710G3B-EC engine rated at 2385 kW/3200 hp at 900 rpm. This design was designated Class 66 within the United Kingdom and the fleet was allotted fleet numbers 66001–250; when sold to operators outside the UK the design was designated JT42CWR.

The first locomotive arrived at Immingham Docks in June 1998 and was immediately sent to Derby for 'type testing' while the second locomotive underwent endurance testing at the Pueblo Test Centre before being shipped to the UK. Once deliveries began they were shipped at the rate of eleven locomotives per month and arrived at Newport Docks where they were craned onto the quayside track, inspected by EWSR engineering staff, then lubricated and fuelled before being accepted into service. In addition to 'working out of the box', each locomotive was expected to provide 95% availability, operate for 180 days between failures, and cover 1.6 million kilometres/ 1 million miles between major rebuilds that were expected to cost £200,000.

The locomotives met the specifications and their reliability led to other UK freight operators ordering examples as they sought to update their fleets; in addition to UK operators, some mainland European companies bought examples, albeit modified with such fittings as air-conditioning to suit local conditions. Production continued until 2011 when a combination of closure of the Ontario plant, due to industrial disputes, and the introduction of new European Union (EU) crash and emission regulations brought production to an end. Further orders placed by GB Railfreight (GBRf) in 2013, however, saw a replacement production line being opened at Muncie, Indiana, from which 66779 was released in 2016 as the final example of the design.

This album provides a brief history of the class in the two decades since 66001 arrived in the UK in June 1998 to show how the design has become the 'jack of all trades' to train operating companies as the locomotives provide both freight and passenger services within the framework of the UK's privatised railway network, and continue to do so as at October 2019.

@ Fred Kerr October 2019

Image 1: DB Cargo (ex EWSR) Class 66/0 66113 rumbles across Whalley Viaduct on 18 November 2016 while working a Mossend–Clitheroe cement service.

Section 1:
Locomotive Operations

1.1: Locomotive Operators

1.1.1: English Welsh & Scottish Railways (EWSR)

When British Railways (BR) introduced its Modernisation Plan in 1954, part of the programme was designed to both encourage UK locomotive manufacturers in, while discouraging American locomotive manufacturers from, supplying the diesel locomotives that had been calculated as being needed to eliminate steam traction from the railway network. This policy was reversed in December 1995 when, as part of the privatisation of BR in 1994, the three major freight companies were bought by a consortium headed by the American railway company Wisconsin Central, that over time became the English Welsh & Scottish Railways (EWSR).

EWSR came into existence as a result of the privatisation of British Railways under the Railways Act 1993 that became effective on 1 April 1994, at which time the two freight operations that had been created in 1988 as a prelude to privatisation were divided into separate companies. Railfreight Distribution (RfD) was divided into Freightliner (to handle container services) and the residual RfD to handle freight services through the Channel Tunnel, while Trainload Freight (TLF) was divided into three companies based on geographical areas to handle bulk movements of aggregates, coal, metal and petroleum products. These companies were Trainload North East, Trainload North West and Trainload South East, which later became Loadhaul, Transrail Freight and Mainline Freight respectively. In addition to these five companies, there was also Rail Express Systems (RES), which had been created in 1991 to handle mail and postal services and charter operations. Once privatisation was enacted, all these freight companies were offered for sale by competitive tender.

The interested parties included an American consortium headed by Wisconsin Central which formed North & South Railways (NSR) to bid for freight operations. Its first success came in December 1995 when it bought RES for £24 million and gained a fleet of 164 locomotives; this was followed in February 1996 by the purchase of the three TLF companies for £225 million thus gaining a further 914 locomotives. The four companies retained their trading names until April 1996 when the EWSR corporate brand was unveiled, followed in July 1996 by the holding company (NSR) changing its name to English Welsh & Scottish Railway Holdings. The three TLF companies were merged into Transrail Freight in October 1996 which was subsequently renamed English Welsh & Scottish Railways Ltd (EWSR).

EWSR was further expanded in December 1996 when it was confirmed as the preferred bidder for the loss-making RfD, which included international container services (via the Channel Tunnel), for the movement of cars and automotive parts and freight services for the Ministry of Defence (MoD). The sale was confirmed in March 1997 when EWSR gained a further 157 locomotives and controlled 90% of the freight market. RfD was renamed English Welsh & Scottish Railways International (EWSI) from 1 December 1998. EWSR made its final purchase on 1 April 1998 when the company bought National Power's rail division to increase its fleet by a further six (Class 59/2) locomotives.

In October 2005 EWSR created Euro Cargo Rail (ECR) in France and transferred sixty of its Class 66 locomotives to create its traction fleet. Foreign interest in the company continued with the announcement in June 2007 that Germany's state railway (Deutsche Bahn (DB)) had agreed to purchase EWSR; the sale was completed in November 2007. DB initially said that EWSR would not be rebranded but, as part of a company restructuring in January 2009, EWSR was rebranded DB-Schenker UK (DBS); in March 2016 the company was renamed once more to DB Cargo UK (DBC).

In 2017 DBC undertook a further fleet review and subsequently offered ten Class 66 locomotives (66008/016/046/058/081/132/141/184/238/250) for sale; these were bought by GB Railfreight (GBRf) in December 2017 and were subsequently reclassified as Class 66/7 and renumbered to 66780–789.

1.1.2: Freightliner

When BR was privatised in 1994, the Freightliner company, currently part of RfD, was established as a separate entity named Freightliner (1995) Limited and offered for sale; in May 1996 the company was bought by its staff as a management buyout funded by private investors.

In 1999 the company gained contracts to operate infrastructure trains on behalf of Railtrack (and later Network Rail as successors in title) and set up a Heavy Haul division to provide motive power. Once established, the new division sought further commercial contracts to service bulk loads such as aggregates, cement, coal, petroleum, scrap metal and waste, resulting in the formation of Freightliner Heavy Haul Ltd in 2001 as a subsidiary company to service the new contracts.

The Freightliner Group was bought by Railinvest Holding Company Ltd, a subsidiary of Arcapita Bank of Bahrain, in June 2008, which subsequently sold a 95% shareholding to the American Genesee & Wyoming Railroad (G&WR) in February 2015 with the remaining 5% to be sold to G&WR by 2020. This arrangement was revised in July 2019 when G&WR offered itself for sale leading to its purchase by a consortium including Brookfield Infrastructure, GIC and Brookfield's institutional partners.

Shortly after deliveries of the EWSR order began, Freightliner ordered a batch of five similar locomotives to service its infrastructure contracts; these were designated Class 66/5 and numbered 66501–505. Even before 66501 had been delivered a further fifteen locomotives, numbered 66506–520, were ordered to both service further infrastructure contracts and replace the ageing Class 47 fleet. Freightliner ordered further batches of locomotives as new contracts were gained and, with the decision taken to standardise future operations on the design, placed sufficient orders to enable the replacement of its ageing Class 47 fleet by 2004 and its Class 57 fleet by 2008.

The Class 66/5 locomotives were delivered in batches as noted at Section 1.2 but, as deliveries began, Freightliner identified a need for locomotives to haul heavier trains and specified a Class 66 design with both lower gearing and maximum speed that was designated Class 66/6 and were also delivered in batches. In 2004 Freightliner took delivery of two locomotives with low emission engines to meet changed European Union (EU) emission regulations; these were designated Class 66/9 and numbered 66951-952. They proved sufficiently successful that subsequent deliveries of all UK orders had the new engine design; for Freightliner this encompassed Class 66/5 66582–599 and 66953–957 and Class 66/6 66623–625.

The fleet has undergone changes with transfers both between companies and to the nascent Polish operation from 2006. Initially the company took over the leases of 66411–420 from Direct Rail Services (DRS) when the latter company surrendered its leases to standardise on the low emission engine-fitted locomotives. Freightliner subsequently surrendered the leases of Class 66/5 66573–577 to Colas Rail and Class 66/5 66578–581 to GB Railfreight while also transferring thirteen locomotives to Poland to provide an initial fleet for the new operation.

1.1.3: New Operators

The legal framework that created the privatisation also permitted new operators to offer rail services, both freight and passenger, and those companies which began operating freight services initially started by using older locomotives either sold by the existing freight companies or hired from preservation groups whose locomotives were certified to operate on the national network. This gave the new companies a chance to establish their business and, once successful, they would obtain Class 66 locomotives to continue developing their services.

There were five companies whose initial success led to their operating Class 66 locomotives (namely Advenza Freight, Colas Rail Freight, Direct Rail Services (DRS), Fastline and GB Railfreight (GBRf)) from which only three managed to become established freight operators. By far the most successful operator has been GBRf and this company took delivery of the final Class 66 locomotive to be built following the imposition over time of EU regulations concerning the exhaust emissions of diesel engines – including railway locomotives. By 2016 the regulations had brought Class 66 construction to an end and GBRf commemorated this at the National Rail Museum in York on 10 May 2016 when Class 66/7 66779 – the final locomotive – was unveiled with a green livery and nameplate similar to that given to Standard Class 9 2-10-0 92220 when Swindon Works dedicated this in 1960 to commemorate the last steam locomotive to be built by BR workshops.

1.1.3.1: Advenza Freight

The company, formed in 2001, gained approval for its safety case in 2002, thus gaining a licence to operate by the Rail Regulator in 2003. Its first operation was a containerised palletised freight service from Barking (Roadways Ltd sidings) to Glasgow (Deanside) that was intended to start in April 2004. The start was delayed by various operating problems, hence their first service finally ran in October 2004 – but only for three weeks as the service failed to attract sufficient custom resulting in the company being offered for sale.

The company was bought by Gloucester-based Cotswold Rail, primarily for its Safety Case, which led to the company gaining a passenger licence in 2006. The company operated four locomotives (Class 47/0 47237; Class 47/3 47375 and Class 57/0 57005/06) which were joined in mid-2009 by four Class 66 locomotives. These had originally been operated by Direct Rail Services (DRS) as Class 66/4 66406-409 but when the leases were transferred to Advenza Freight they were reclassified Class 66/8 and renumbered 66841-844. Their service life with Advenza Freight was short-lived as HM Revenue and Customs (HMRC) wound up the company in October 2009 due to unpaid taxes and the locomotive leases were transferred to Colas Rail Freight where they retained both their Class 66/8 classifications and fleet numbers.

1.1.3.2: Colas Rail Freight

Colas Rail Freight is the UK subsidiary of the French company SECO (Societé d'Études et de Construction d'Outillage) that had been bought by road building company COLAS. Although based in France, the group had UK subsidiaries, and in January 2008 COLAS merged its SECO Rail operations with its AMEC-Spie rail subsidiary to form Colas Rail; the new company included the purchase of the On Track Plant (OTP) division of Carillion Rail.

The first contract gained by Colas Rail Freight was the haulage of the Kronospan timber flow from Carlisle to Chirk which was initially powered by hired-in locomotives until it could obtain its own locomotive fleet. This was achieved by the purchase of three Class 47/7 locomotives (47727/739/747) and Class 56 locomotives to power its increasing number of haulage contracts. The company took up the leases of Class 66/8 66841–844 when Advenza Freight was wound up by HMRC plus that of Class 66/4 66410 from DRS which was reclassified Class 66/8 and renumbered 66845. These five locomotives were sub-leased from GB Railfreight (GBRf) but, during 2011, the leases were terminated when the locomotives were re-called by GBRf to be reclassified Class 66/7 and renumbered 66742–746. Colas Rail Freight subsequently took up the leases of Freightliner's Class 66/5 66573–577 as replacement which were reclassified Class 66/8 and renumbered 66846–850.

1.1.3.3: Direct Rail Services (DRS)

DRS was created at the privatisation of BR in April 1994 when the firm of British Nuclear Fuels (BNF) decided to operate its own train services for the movement of nuclear flasks to and from Sellafield for which, following the transfer of BNF to the Nuclear Decommissioning Authority in 1994, it assembled a fleet of Class 20 and Class 37 locomotives to provide motive power. With this locomotive fleet the company looked to expand and gained contracts with the Malcolm Group in 2002 to provide services between Grangemouth and Daventry for which a fleet of ten Class 66 locomotives were ordered. These were classified Class 66/4 and numbered 66401–410 when delivered to the company's dedicated base at Carlisle Kingmoor in 2003. As the company gained further contracts, additional locomotives were ordered resulting in the delivery of 66411–420 in 2006, 66421–66430 in 2007, and a final batch 66431–434 in 2008. Following the successful introduction of the low-emission locomotives in 2004, classified Class 66/9 and numbered 66951/2 by Freightliner, 66411–434 were built to the lower-emission specification.

The DRS fleet of Class 66 locomotives has fluctuated; an early change came when Fastline Rail (see 1.1.3.4) ceased trading in March 2010 and its Class 66/3 fleet (66301–305) was placed into store at Kingmoor; the leases were subsequently taken up by DRS. Shortly after, the leases on 66401–410 came up for review and DRS elected to release them having decided to standardise on the low-emission locomotives. 66401–405 were re-leased to GB Railfreight (GBRf) to become Class 66/7 66733–737 while 66406–409 were re-leased to Advenza Freight to become Class 66/8 66841–844 but, on the liquidation of that company, consequently re-leased to Colas Rail Freight (with the addition of 66410 that became Class 66/8 66845). 66841–845 were on sub-lease from GBRf and when GBRf recalled them to become Class 66/7 66742–746, Colas Rail Freight took up the leases of Freightliner's Class 66/5 66573–577 as replacement to become 6618 66846–66850.

In a later review DRS elected to surrender the leases of 66411–420 which were taken up by Freightliner; this allowed the latter company to transfer thirteen of its Class 66 fleet to Poland to start up its nascent business in coal movements. In October 2018 the delivery of Class 68 and Class 88 locomotives, allied to the downturn in traffic flows resulting from the cessation of coal traffic when coal-fired power stations were closed as a result of government policies regarding carbon emission limits, is expected to lead to further reviews of its locomotive fleet.

1.1.3.4: Fastline Rail

Fastline Rail was initially a management buyout of Eastern Track Renewals that was completed in 1996 then subsequently bought by Jarvis which resurrected the name as a railway freight operation. Its first contract was to haul containers between Doncaster and the Isle of Grain for which it bought three refurbished Class 56 locomotives that were designated Class 56/3 and numbered 56301–303; these were later supplemented by a further duo of refurbished locomotives that were numbered 56311–312.

The next major contract was a series to supply coal to Ratcliffe Power Station, initially from Hatfield Colliery then from Daw Mill Colliery followed by further workings from Daw Mill to Cottam Power Station, Immingham Dock to Ironbridge Power Station, and Liverpool Bulk Terminal to Ratcliffe Power Station. To power these services a fleet of five Class 66 locomotives was ordered; classified Class 66/3 and numbered 66301–305 they were delivered during 2008.

Jarvis entered administration in March 2010 thus forcing Fastline Rail to cease operating – just as the company was negotiating with DRS for the lease of Class 66/4 66434. DRS had already repainted 66434 into Fastline livery but, on the cessation of operations, retained the locomotive replete with its 'new' livery while the Class 66/3 fleet was placed into store at Kingmoor Depot. During 2011 DRS took up the leases of the Class 66/3 fleet, initially operating them in Fastline livery before repainting them into the corporate DRS livery.

1.1.3.5: GB Railfreight (GBRf)

GB Railfreight was founded in 1999 and began operations with a contract to operate infrastructure services for Railtrack, based at Whitemoor yard near March for which a fleet of seven Class 66 locomotives was ordered; these were classified Class 66/7, numbered 66701–707 and based at a new depot at Peterborough. This was followed in 2002 by its first intermodal contract on behalf of Mediterranean Shipping Company (MSC) to move containers between Felixstowe and Selby and a contract to transport gypsum on behalf of British Gypsum.

As further contracts were gained, the company standardised on the Class 66 design, although willing to use heritage traction where appropriate for short-term contracts. Whilst batches of locomotives were initially ordered to service specific contracts, the increase in contracts quickly led to the fleet becoming operated as 'common user', but such was the demand for locomotives that, in addition to obtaining locomotives directly from the builder, the company took up leases from other companies and imported locomotives from the European mainland. The imported locomotives were converted to the UK specification before being numbered into the 667xx number range and entering service.

The fleet livery has also reflected the changes in ownership of the company since its inception, although there has been no change in management – as at October 2019 being led by John Smith as Managing Director. The company was first bought by First Group in August 2003 and rebranded First GBRf as First Group sought to expand operations into East Anglia when the East Anglian passenger franchise came up for renewal. First Group's franchise bid failed and in May 2010 GBRf was offered for sale; it was bought by Europorte in June 2011, resulting in a reversion to its original name and a revised company livery. In October 2016 the company was sold once more to EQT Partners, a private equity group that invests in commercial businesses on a long-term basis, and became part of the Hector Rail operation albeit still operating independently within the UK. In early July 2019 Hector Rail sold the company to Infracapital, an unlisted infrastructure equity arm of M&G Prudential.

1.2: Locomotive Deliveries

The Class 66 deliveries to the UK were made over a period of eighteen years, excluding the additional locomotives imported by GBRf from European sources. The delivery dates for the locomotives to their original UK operators is noted under:

66001–250	EWSR	1998–2000
a. 60 locomotives transferred to EWS Cargo in France		
b. 66048 scrapped after accident at Carrbridge 04/01/2010		
c. 10 locomotives sold to GBRf in January 2018 [66008/016/046/058/081/132/141/184/238/250: =66780–789]		
66301–305	Fastline	2008
a. Leases taken up by DRS during 2011		
66401–410	DRS	2003
a. 5 locomotives transferred to GBRf [66401-405:=66733-737]		
b. 4 locomotives transferred to Advenza Railfreight [66406-409:=66841-844]		
c. 1 locomotive transferred to GBRf sub-leased to Colas Rail Freight [66410:=66845]		
66411–420	DRS	2006
a. 10 locomotives transferred to Freightliner [66411- 66420]		
b. 3 locomotives subsequently exported to Poland [66411/412/417]		
66421–430	DRS	2007
66431–434	DRS	2008
66501–505	Freightliner	1999
66506–520	Freightliner	2000
66521–526	Freightliner	2000
a. 66521 written off in Heck accident 28/02/2001		
66526–531	Freightliner	2001
66532–537	Freightliner	2001
66538–543	Freightliner	2001
66544–553	Freightliner	2001
66554	Freightliner	2002
66555–566	Freightliner	2002
66567–574	Freightliner	2003
a. 2 locomotives to Colas Rail Freight [66573-574:=66846-847]		
66575–577	Freightliner	2004
a. 3 locomotives to Colas Rail Freight [66575-577:=66848-850]		
66578–581	Freightliner	2005
a. 4 locomotives transferred to GBRf [66578-581:=66738-741]		
66582–594	Freightliner	2007
a. 4 locomotives exported to Poland [66582/583/584/586]		
66595–599	Freightliner	2008
a. 1 locomotive exported to Poland [66595]		
66601–606	Freightliner	2000
66607–612	Freightliner	2002
a. 4 locomotives exported to Poland [66607/609/611/612]		
66613–618	Freightliner	2003
66619–622	Freightliner	2005
66623–625	Freightliner	2007
a. 2 locomotives exported to Poland [66624/625]		
66701–707	GBRf	2001
66708–712	GBRf	2002
66713–717	GBRf	2003
66718–722	GBRf	2006
66723–727	GBRf	2006
66728–732	GBRf	2008
66733–737	ex DRS (66401-405)	
a. 66734 written off in Loch Treig landslide 28/06/2012		
66738–741	ex Freightliner (66578-581)	
66742–746	ex Colas Rail Freight (66841-45)	
66747–749	GBRf	(2008)
a. bought from Crossrail AG (Holland) in 2012		
66750–751	GBRf	(2003)
a. leased from European ROSCO in 2013		
66752–772	GBRf	2014
66773–779	GBRf	2016
66780–789	ex EWSR (66008/016/046/058/081/132/141/184/238/250)	1998–2000
66790–792	GBRf	(2019)
a. leased from Sweden through Beacon Rail in June 2019		
66841–844	ex Advenza Railfreight (66406–409)	
a. 4 locomotives transferred to GBRf sub-leased to Colas Rail Freight [66841-844]		
b. 4 locomotives returned to GBRf [66841-44:=66742-745]		
66845		ex DRS (66410)
a. 1 locomotive transferred to GBRf sub-leased to Colas Rail Freight [66845]		
b. 1 locomotive returned to GBRf [66845:=66746]		
66846–850	ex Freightliner (66573–577)	
66951–952	Freightliner	2004
66953–957	Freightliner	2008
a. 1 locomotive exported to Poland [66954]		

1.3: Customer Liveries

Each operating company had a corporate livery and, in the early days of Class 66 operation, a commitment to a customer was normally marked by applying a dedicated name to a locomotive; this would be unveiled to public display by the customer in a celebratory event at either his railway centre or a location where the company's traffic was to be handled.

This changed in 2002 when GB Railfreight (GBRf) marked its first container contract with Mediterranean Shipping Company (MSC) by naming its Class 66/7 locomotive 66709, the first locomotive of the batch ordered to service the new contract, *Joseph Arnold Davies* and applying an MSC-related livery. The concept was repeated in 2006 when GBRf marked its involvement with London Transport's Metronet infrastructure contact by applying a corporate branding to the five dedicated locomotives, 66718-722, that had been ordered for the contract. Since then the use of dedicated liveries to mark the gaining/renewal of contracts has become a more common practice in the operation of the class 66 fleet by the other freight companies.

1.4: Operating Regions

The operation of the fleet by various operators has been reflected within this album by division into ten regions, allied to the rail passenger timetable, as defined in the 1970s by the *Diesel Enthusiast's Pocket Guide* produced by Bradford Barton. This guide gave mileages for all rail lines within the country and was divided into ten volumes related to the passenger timetables for easy reference.

1. Eastern Region South: Tables 1–24 – routes within the area east of ECML between London Kings Cross to Peterborough.
2. Yorkshire and Lincolnshire: Tables 26–34; 40.
3. Northern England: Tables 26; 31; 36–37; 41–44; 48;65; 108; 110–113 – routes within the area north of Preston to Floriston (including the Furness Coast) in the west and north of Leeds/York to the River Tweed in the east.
4. LM Region South: Tables 18; 30; 52–56; 59; 61–62; 64–66; 69–70; 80–81 – routes south of Manchester encompassed by the west Coast Main Line (WCML) to the east and the Midland Main Line (MML) to the west.
5. LM Region North West: Tables 33; 39; 58; 65; 81–83; 91–108 – routes within the area bounded to the north by a line from Blackpool to Leeds and to the south by a line from Chester/Crewe to Sheffield including the freight lines around Buxton – routes west of a line from Crewe to Newport.
7. Thames – Cotswolds: Tables 56; 67; 71; 114–116; 118–121; 123; 126–127; 133 – routes encompassed by Birmingham to Bristol to the west; Bristol to Paddington to the south; and Paddington to Birmingham (GWR) to the east.
8. Wessex and West Country: Tables 123; 132–133; 135–137; 139–140; 142–145; 156; 158–160; 165–167 – routes south of a line from Paddington to Bristol via Berks & Hants line and west of the line from Woking to Portsmouth.
9. South & South East: Tables 124; 147–150; 152; 156; 175–176; 178–179; 182; 184; 186; 189; 195; 198–201; 205–207; 210; 212–213 – routes encompassed by a line from Reading to Havant in the west; Reading to Waterloo in the north; and all lines in Kent and Sussex.
10. Scotland: Tables 26; 65; 216–243 – all lines north of a line from the River Tweed to the Solway Firth.

Section 2:
UK Regions

2.1: Eastern Region South

This region encompasses all lines east of (and including) the East Coast Main Line (ECML) between London Kings Cross to Peterborough.

Image 2: A trio of GBRf Class 66/7 locomotives sees 66710 leading 66705 *Golden Jubilee* and 66706 *Nene Valley* as they prepare to leave Whitemoor yard on 21 June 2004 en route to their home base at Peterborough.

Image 3: GBRf Class 66/7 66715 *VALOUR In memory of all Railway Employees who gave their lives for their country* approaches Whitemoor yard on 21 June 2004 while working a local infrastructure service from March East yard.

Image 4: GBRf Class 66/7 66754 *Northampton Saints* curves off the cross-country Peterborough/Bury St Edmunds route onto the Great Eastern Main Line at Haughley on 11 August 2016 while working a (Rotherham) Masborough–Felixstowe container service.

Top Left – Image 5: A major engineering renewal at Ilford sees GBRf Class 66/7 66709 *Joseph Arnold Davies* working in top 'n' tail mode with sister locomotive 66704 as they wait to deposit ballast on 24 July 2005 while …

Below Left – Image 6: … sister locomotive 66716 *Willesden Traincare Centre* awaits departure to Whitemoor with spent ballast.

Right – Image 7: The previous night EWSR Class 66/0 66091 was stabled on site as staff began to take up the old track that was being replaced.

Image 8: DB Cargo (ex EWSR) Class 66/0 66126 eases through Finsbury Park on 13 May 2017 while working a Cottam Power Station–Acton service.

Image 9: EWSR Class 66/0 66190 descends Brentwood bank on 14 May 2004 while working a Chelmsford–Mountsorrel Civil Engineer's service comprising the High Output Ballast Cleaner (HOBC) trainset.

Image 10: Freightliner Class 66/5 66534 *OCL Express* curves past Gospel Oak on 24 August 2010 while working a (Birmingham) Lawley St–Felixstowe container service.

A major traffic flow within the region is that of container services to/from Felixstowe Docks, many of which traverse the outskirts of London hence crossing the River Stour at Manningtree.

Top Right – Image 11: GBRf Class 66/7 66716 heads south on 23 June 2004 while working a Felixstowe–Hams Hall service.

Below Left – Image 12: Freightliner Class 66/5 66542 heads south on 23 June 2004 while working an Ipswich–Tilbury service.

Below Right – Image 13: EWSR Class 66/0 66200 heads south on 22 June 2004 while working a Felixstowe–Harwich 'Enterprise' service.

Image 14: GBRf Class 66/7 66768 passes Diss on 11 August 2016 while working a North Walsham–Harwich condensate service. North Walsham is a collection point for gas condensate from oil pipelines, which is transferred by rail to Harwich for further processing thus providing a regular and valuable traffic within the region.

Top Left – Image 15: Freightliner Class 66/5 66505 descends Brentwood bank on 14 May 2014 while working an Ipswich–Tilbury container service.

Below Left – Image 16: Freightliner Class 66/5 66955 powers through Gidea Park on 12 May 2017 while working a Bristol–Felixstowe container service.

Right – Image 17: GBRf Class 66/7 66716 *Willesden Traincare Depot* curves into Manningtree on 26 July 2006 while working a Felixstowe–Hams Hall container service.

2.2: Yorkshire & Lincolnshire

This region provides a wide variety of freight services within the respective county boundaries, many of which are geared to the supply of coal to the Aire Valley power stations and the importing of raw materials through Immingham Docks to feed the demands of the steelworks at Scunthorpe. The closure of the coal-fired power stations has had a consequence on freight services as freight companies seek new markets to develop as replacement for the fast-disappearing coal trains.

Image 18: EWSR Class 66/0 66115 curves through Brocklesby Junction on 6 January 2004 while working a Scunthorpe–Immingham merry-go-round (mgr) service.

Image 19: GBRf Class 66/7 66780 (originally delivered to EWSR as Class 66/0 66008) bears Cemex company livery as it climbs past Embsay on 26 October 2018 while working a Hull Dairycoates–Rylstone Tilcon Quarry aggregates service to collect another load. The recent development of aggregate quarrying in this part of North Yorkshire has helped counteract the loss of coal freight services through the closure of coal-fired power stations.

Image 20: EWSR Class 66/0 66198 curves past Milford Junction on 3 February 2003 while setting up a trainset in Milford Sidings yard.

Image 21: Freightliner Class 66/5 66559 departs from Milford Sidings on 3 February 2003 while working an mgr service to Eggborough Power Station.

Image 22: EWSR Class 66/0 66005 departs from Milford Sidings on 3 February 2003 while working an mgr service to Ayr.

Top Left – Image 23: EWSR Class 66/0 66217 passes Crowle on 2 June 2004 while working an Immingham–Margam steel service.

Below Left – Image 24: DB Cargo (Ex EWSR) Class 66/0 66185 passes Colton Junction on 6 July 2016 while working a Lackenby–Scunthorpe steel service.

Below Right – Image 25: EWSR Class 66/0 66247 approaches Colton Junction on 9 June 2005 while working a Scunthorpe–Lackenby steel service.

Image 26: EWSR Class 66/0 66058 drifts through Crowle on 2 June 2004 while working an Ashton–Lindsey Oil Refinery petroleum service.

Image 27: DB Schenker (ex EWSR) Class 66/0 66119 heads south out of York at Copmanthorpe on 27 August 2013 while working a Tees Dock–Aldwarke steel service.

Image 28: **GBRf Class 66/7 66703** *Doncaster PSB 1981–2002* **curves through Doncaster on 19 January 2012 while working an Immingham–Eggborough Power Station mgr service.**

Image 29: Freightliner Class 66/5 66578 passes Colton Junction on 9 June 2005 while working a Wilton–Leeds container service.

Image 30: GBRf Class 66/7 66712 passes Ellergill House on 16 August 2006 while traversing the Grassington Branch with a Swinden Quarry–Bury St Edmunds aggregates service.

Image 31: GBRf Class 66/7 66747, imported from Germany and still bearing the livery of its original operator, passes Copmanthorpe, on the outskirts of York, on 16 April 2014 while working a Drax Power Station–Tyne Dock mgr service.

Image 32: GBRf Class 66/7 66740 (originally delivered to Freightliner as Class 66/5 66580) passes Copmanthorpe on 26 October 2012 while working a Tyne Dock–Cottam Power Station mgr service.

Image 33: EWSR Class 66/0 66229 curves away from Hellifield on 16 December 2006 while working a Hunterston–Drax Power Station mgr service.

Image 34: GBRf Class 66/7 66715 *VALOUR In memory of all Railway Employees who gave their lives for their country* heads north past Overton Lane on 29 February 2016 while working a Ferrybridge Power Station–North Blyth coal service.

Image 35: DB Schenker (ex EWSR) Class 66/0 66075 passes Heck Ings on 10 July 2008 as it passes under the ECML while working a New Cumnock–Drax Power Station mgr service.

Image 36: Freightliner Class 66/6 66607 passes Heck Ings on 10 July 2008 while working a Drax Power Station–Tunstead limestone service.

Image 37: GBRf Class 66/7 66714 *Cromer Lifeboat* passes Cracoe on 28 June 2006 while traversing the Grassington Branch with a Swinden Quarry–Bury St Edmunds aggregates service.

Image 38: Freightliner Class 66/5 66544 approaches Colton Junction on 6 July 2016 while working a Mountsorrel–Tyne Yard Civil Engineer's aggregates service.

Top Right – Image 39: DB Cargo (ex EWSR) Class 66/0 66047 *Maritime International TWO* bears a customer-based livery as it passes Doncaster on 7 May 2019 while working a Wakefield–Felixstowe container service.

Below Left – Image 40: GBRf Class 66/7 66709 *Joseph Arnold Davies* bears MSC company livery as it crosses the Selby Swing Bridge on 2 December 2003 while working a Selby–Felixstowe container service.

Below Right – Image 41: GBRf Class 66/7 66704 *Colchester Power Signalbox* reverses its Felixstowe–Selby container service into Potters Yard on 8 September 2009.

2.3: Northern England
This region is based around three main lines – namely the West Coast Main Line (including the Furness Coast) between Preston and Carlisle; the Settle and Carlisle route from Hellifield to Carlisle (including the Ribble Valley route from Blackburn to Hellifield); and the East Coast Main Line (including the north-east coastal route) north of York.

2.3.1: West Coast Main Line
This route is part of the electrified West Coast Main Line (WCML) with diesel traction used for services working to/from the minor and non-electrified routes.

Image 42: DB Schenker (ex EWSR) Class 66/0 66001, the first UK locomotive of the Class 66 fleet, curves through Euxton on 10 June 2013 while working a Carlisle–Basford Hall Civil Engineer's service.

The WCML route includes the climb of Shap through the northern Lake District where, in steam days, trains were banked from Tebay to Shap Summit; today's traction has no need of assistance as seen at Greenholme where …

Top Right – Image 43: … Freightliner Class 66/5 66545 headed north on 21 August 2010 while working a Fiddlers Ferry Power Station–Hunterston mgr service.

Below Left – Image 44: … EWSR Class 66/0 66162 headed north on 18 April 2007 while working a Warrington Arpley–Ayr mgr service.

Below Right – Image 45: … EWSR Class 66/0 66222 headed north on 3 April 2004 while working a Burngullow–Irvine china clay service.

Image 46: DRS Class 66/4 66411 *Eddie the Engine* curves through Oubeck on 2 November 2006 while working the daily Daventry–Grangemouth TescoLiner. Of note is the Stobart company livery borne by the locomotive that commemorated the awarding of the logistics contract to Stobart and the subsequent choice of DRS as the hauler.

Image 47: DRS Class 66/4 66429 + 66434 curve through Oubeck on 10 July 2013 while working the daily Daventry–Mossend TescoLiner. Note that 66434 carries the livery of the Malcolm Group – commemorating another customer then served by DRS.

Image 48: Freightliner Class 66/5 66549 climbs to Beckfoot on 25 September 2004 while working a Mossend–Crewe Gresty Lane automotive service.

Image 49: Freightliner Class 66/5 66586 curves through Beckfoot on 4 April 2007 while working a Workington–Basford Hall Civil Engineer's service.

Although handling a much reduced traffic level, Workington Docks still maintains a regular rail service.

Left – Image 50: DB Schenker (ex EWSR) Class 66/0 66030 curves through Maryport on 1 December 2009 while working a Workington–Carlisle container service.

Below – Image 51: DB Schenker (ex EWSR) Class 66/0 66171 passes Siddick on 25 May 2010 while working a Workington–Carlisle container service.

Image 52: Freightliner Class 66/5 66507 climbs through Greenholme as it ascends Shap on 30 January 2003 while working a Shap Quarry–Carlisle Kingmoor aggregates service that had reversed at Tebay.

Image 53: Freightliner Class 66/5 66525 climbs through Greenholme as it ascends Shap on 16 April 2010 while working a Fiddlers Ferry Power Station–Chalmerston mgr service.

Night scenes at Carlisle, where crew changes take place, include …

Image 54: … DRS (ex Fastline) Class 66/3 66304 on 15 November 2012 while working a Grangemouth–Daventry container service.

Image 55: … Colas Rail Freight Class 66/8 66850 (originally delivered to Freightliner as Class 66/5 66577) on 15 November 2012 while working a Sinfin (Derby)–Grangemouth petroleum service.

Image 56: … DRS Class 66/4 66403 on 16 June 2004 while working a Grangemouth–Daventry container service.

Image 57: … DB Schenker (ex EWSR) Class 66/0 66069 on 17 July 2015 while working a Cardiff–Mossend 'Enterprise' service.

Image 58: DRS Class 66/4 66410 curves through Beckfoot on 28 July 2006 while working a Coatbridge–Daventry container service.

The Morecambe–Heysham branch has an infrequent freight service comprising a weekly service of flasks between Sellafield and Heysham Power Station as noted on 2 November 2006 when …

Top Left – Image 59: … DRS Class 66/4 66414 arrived in top 'n' tail mode with sister locomotive 66417 and …

Below Left – Image 60: … proceeded to shunt the yard during the transfer process.

Below Right – Image 61: The branch was visited by an enthusiast's charter train on 30 May 2005 when Freightliner Class 66/6 66608 was noted coming off the branch at Morecambe Ground Frame working a Heysham–Swindon return charter in top 'n' tail mode with Freightliner Class 66/9 66951.

2.3.2: Settle and Carlisle Route

This route nominally begins at Settle Junction and cuts through the Pennines to Carlisle where it once formed the northern link of the Midland Railway's Anglo-Scottish main line. It is now much reduced in importance but is also associated with the Ribble Valley route that runs between Blackburn to Hellifield where it joins the ex-Midland Railway route as it continues the short distance to Settle Junction.

An important source of traffic is the Cement Plant at Clitheroe which generates a service to both Mossend via the Settle & Carlisle route and Avonmouth via the WCML.

Right – Image 62: DB Cargo (ex EWSR) Class 66/0 66113 crosses Whalley Viaduct on 18 November 2016 while working a Mossend–Clitheroe service, diverted from its normal route by engineering work.

Below – Image 63: DB Schenker (ex EWSR) Class 66/0 66093 propels its trainset under the loading bay at Clitheroe on 2 March 2011.

Top Left – Image 64: DB Schenker (ex EWSR) Class 66/0 66144 sets back its Mossend–Clitheroe service into the cement company siding on 19 August 2009.

Below Left – Image 65: DB Schenker (ex EWSR) Class 66/0 66100 propels its Clitheroe–Mossend service from the cement plant onto the network line as a prelude to working forward on 9 April 2008.

Below Right – Image 66: DB Schenker (ex EWSR) Class 66/0 66113 propels its trainset under the loading bay at Clitheroe on 31 January 2014.

Top Left – Image 67: EWSR Class 66/0 66174 curves through Clitheroe on 12 May 2007 while working a Burngullow–Irvine china clay service, diverted from its normal WCML route by engineering works.

Below Left – Image 68: DB Schenker (ex EWSR) Class 66/0 66227 approaches Whalley on 30 April 2010 while working a Carlisle–Basford Hall infrastructure service.

Right – Image 69: Colas Rail Freight Class 66//8 66843 (originally delivered to DRS as Class 66/4 66408 then re-leased to Advenza Freight to become Class 66/8 66843) passes under Clitheroe Castle on July 14 2011 while working a Carlisle–Chirk timber service.

Image 70: DRS Class 66/4 66423 has Freightliner Class 66/6 66602 in the consist of its Carlisle–Basford Hall Civil Engineer's service as it passes through Whalley on 28 May 2015.

Image 71: EWSR Class 66/0 66013 curves through Langcliffe on 14 April 2007 while working a Burngullow–Irvine china clay service, diverted from its normal WCML route by engineering works.

Image 72: EWSR Class 66/0 66164 curves off Ribblehead Viaduct on 6 September 2007 while working a Hunterston–Ratcliffe Power Station mgr service.

Image 73: DB Schenker (ex EWSR) Class 66/0 66099 curves off Ribblehead Viaduct on 11 August 2010 while working a Carlisle–Basford Hall Civil Engineer's service.

Image 74: GBRf Class 66/7 66706 *Nene Valley* climbs through Ribblehead on 20 May 2010 while working a Drax Power Station–Newbiggin gypsum service.

Image 75: GBRf Class 66/7 66722 *Sir Edward Watkin*, replete with London Transport Metronet branding, curves off Ribblehead Viaduct on 11 December 2008 while working a Newbiggin–West Burton Power Station gypsum service.

Image 76: GBRf Class 66/7 66708 *Jayne* climbs up to Ais Gill on 3 June 2006 while working a West Burton Power Station–Newbiggin gypsum service.

Image 77: Freightliner Class 66/5 66559 pilots failed Freightliner Class 70 70011 across Ribblehead Viaduct on 24 May 2012 while working a Killoch–Fiddlers Ferry Power Station mgr service.

Image 78: GBRf Class 66/7 66709 *Joseph Arnold Davies*, bearing MSC company livery, curves across Ribblehead Viaduct on 10 June 2006 while working a West Burton Power Station–Newbiggin gypsum service.

Top Left – Image 79: Colas Rail Freight Class 66/8 66848 (originally delivered to Freightliner as Class 66/5 66575) curves off Ribblehead Viaduct on 14 June 2012 while working a Carlisle–Chirk timber service.

During autumn, when poor weather results in limited adhesion, the network rail tracks are treated with chemicals sprayed from Rail Head Treatment Trains (RHTT) and the Settle & Carlisle route is one of those that sees the RHTT train in action during daylight hours.

Below Left – Image 80: DRS Class 66/4 66420 leads sister locomotive 66424 at Helwith Bridge on 30 October 2007 as they head north on the Settle Junction–Carlisle leg of an RHTT diagram

Below Right – Image 81: DRS Class 66/4 66412 leads sister locomotive 66413 at Settle Junction on 30 November 2006 as they head north on the Settle Junction–Carlisle leg of an RHTT diagram.

2.3.3: East Coast Routes

This route mainly covers the East Coast Main Line (ECML) north of York to the River Tweed, south of Berwick-upon-Tweed, and includes both the coastal industrial belt between the Rivers Tees and Tyne and the Northumbrian coast north of Newcastle.

Image 82: GBRf Class 66/7 66717 *Good Old Boy* crosses the River Wansbeck at Black Close on 19 April 2011 while working a Tyne Dock–Lynemouth mgr service.

Image 83: Freightliner Class 66/6 66613 curves through Morpeth on 11 March 2004 while working a Seaham–Oxwellmains cement service.

Top Right – Image 84: Freightliner Class 66/5 66544 eases through Tees Yard on 5 November 2003 while working a Redcar–Cottam Power Station mgr service.

Below Left – Image 85: Freightliner Class 66/5 66541 is stabled in Wilton FLT on 4 November 2003 while its train for Leeds is loaded with containers.

Below Right – Image 86: Freightliner Class 66/6 66610 stands in Seaham Dock on 6 November 2003 while its load of cement is discharged before returning to Oxwellmains.

Image 87: EWSR Class 66/0 66037 shunts its trainset in Tees Yard on 5 November 2003 before working a Tees Yard–Redcar mgr service.

Image 88: **GBRf Class 66/7 66726** *Sheffield Wednesday* curves past Freemans Level Crossing on 19 April 2011 while working a North Blyth–Fort William aluminium service having previously …

Image 89: … waited to depart from North Blyth loading point after its trainset had been loaded.

Image 90: GBRf Class 66/7 66721 *Harry Beck* enters North Blyth Loading Yard on 19 April 2011 with an mgr service from Tyne Dock.

2.4: LM Region South

This region encompasses the West Coast Main Line (WCML) south of Manchester to the west and the Midland Main Line (MML) to the east but excluding both the Hope Valley and Peak Forest routes.

Image 91: Freightliner Class 66/5 66522 curves through Slindon on 12 August 2003 while working a Southampton–Basford Hall automotive service.

Image 92: EWSR Class 66/0 66024 approaches Stockport on 1 November 2003 while working a Roxby–Northenden Greater Manchester Council (GMC) waste service.

Top Right – Image 93: EWSR Class 66/0 66061 curves through Clay Cross on 13 May 2005 while working a Margam–Lackenby steel service.

Below Left – Image 94: EWSR Class 66/0 66042 *Lafarge Buddon Wood* speeds through Tupton on 5 July 2006 while working a Lackenby–Margam steel service.

Below Right – Image 95: DB Schenker (ex EWSR) Class 66/0 66155 passes Aston on 16 May 2012 while working a Hams Hall–Ipswich container service.

Top Left – Image 96: DB Schenker (ex EWSR) Class 66/0 66136 curves through Heamies Bridge on 27 March 2012 while working a Halewood–Southampton Docks automotive service.

Below Left – Image 97: Freightliner Class 66/5 66540 pilots sister locomotive 66534 *OCL Express* as they approach Stockport on 1 November 2003 while working a Trafford Park–Southampton Maritime container service.

Below Right – Image 98: GBRf Class 66/7 66741 (originally delivered to Freightliner as Class 66/5 66581) provides insurance to GBRf Class 92 92028 *Saint Saens* as it approaches Manchester Oxford Road on 3 September 2014 while working a Trafford Park–Felixstowe container service that was testing the Class 92 locomotive after a return to service following a lengthy period in store.

Image 99: Freightliner Class 66/5 66541 has Freightliner Class 86/6 86627+86610 dead in transit as it curves through Bushey on 11 May 2004 while working a Hams Hall–Ipswich container service.

Image 100: EWSR Class 66/0 66130 heads north past Carpenders Park on 11 May 2004 while working a Wembley–Hams Hall automotive service.

Image 101: DB Cargo (ex EWSR) Class 66/0 66013 drifts past South Kenton on 11 May 2017 while working a Dowlow–Southampton aggregates service.

Image 102: EWSR Class 66/0 66083 curves through Bushey on 11 May 2004 while working a Hams Hall–Wembley container service.

Image 103: DB Cargo (ex EWSR) Class 66/0 66113 eases out of Cricklewood on 15 May 2017 while working a Cricklewood–Calvert waste service.

Image 104: EWSR Class 66/0 66238 approaches Harrow and Wealdstone on 11 May 2004 while working a Bletchley–Wembley Civil Engineer's service.

Image 105: DB Cargo (ex EWSR) Class 66/0 66132 descends through Portway on 8 March 2016 while working a Margam–Redcar mgr service.

Scenes from Kidderminster include …

Top Left – Image 106: … DB Schenker (ex EWSR) Class 66/0 66188 passing on 3 October 2014 while working a Margam–Round Oak steel service. In the background preserved Class 50 50017 *Royal Oak* stands at the head of stock on the Severn Valley Railway.

Below Left – Image 107: … DB Cargo (ex EWSR) Class 66/0 66188 speeding past on 17 May 2019 while working a Round Oak–Margam steel service.

Below Right – Image 108: … DB Cargo (ex EWSR) Class 66/0 66221 speeding past on 14 October 2018 while working a Round Oak–Margam steel service.

Top Right – Image 109: DB Schenker (ex EWSR) Class 66/0 66047 approaches Cossington on 19 March 2013 while working a Doncaster–Mountsorrel aggregates service that had reversed at Syston.

Below Left – Image 110: DB Schenker (ex EWSR) Class 66/0 66210 curves through Clay Cross on 9 November 2007 while working a Wolverhampton–Doncaster steel service.

Below Right – Image 111: EWSR Class 66/0 66181 weaves through Great Bowden on 7 June 2004 while working an Elstow–Mountsorrel aggregates service.

Top Left – Image 112: Fastline Class 66/3 66302 curves through Portway on 28 January 2009 while working a Ratcliffe Power Station–Daw Mill Colliery mgr service.

Below Left – Image 113: DB Schenker (ex EWSR) Class 66/0 66131 curves through Portway on 24 April 2013 while working a Toton–Bescot infrastructure service.

Below Right – Image 114: GBRf Class 66/7 66719 *Metro-Land* curves through Portway on 28 January 2009 while working a Ratcliffe Power Station–Portbury mgr service.

Image 115: GBRf Class 66/7 66715 VALOUR *In memory of all railway employees who gave their lives for their country* approaches Cossington on 19 March 2013 while working a Wellingborough–Mountsorrel aggregates service.

Image 116: Shortly after DRS Class 66/4 66406 had been re-leased to Advenza Freight, where it became Class 66/8 66841, it made a visit to the preserved Barrow Hill Roundhouse where it became a display item during a Diesel Gala event. Bearing its new livery and branding, 66841 arrives at Barrow Hill on 8 August 2009 to start its visit.

Image 117: **Freightliner Class 66/5 66544 poses on the turntable at the preserved Barrow Hill Roundhouse on 6 October 2002 when it was a guest locomotive during a Diesel Gala event held at the site.**

2.5: LM Region North West

This region encompasses routes within the area bounded to the north by the Blackpool–Copy Pit–Leeds line and to the south by the Chester–Crewe–Manchester–Hope Valley–Sheffield line and includes the freight workings around the Peak Forest/Buxton area.

Image 118: Having been purchased by GBRf from DB Cargo to become GBRf Class 66/7 66780, ex EWSR Class 66/0 66008 retains the livery and branding of its original operator as it passes Balshaw Lane Junction on 25 July 2018 while working the Wembley–Irvine leg of the weekly Antwerp–Irvine china clay service.

Scenes from Euxton, located on the WCML south of Preston:

Top Right – Image 119: GBRf Class 66/7 66744 was originally delivered to DRS as Class 66/4 66408 then re-leased to Advenza Freight to become Class 66/8 66843 before being leased to GB Railfreight but subleased to Colas Rail Freight; when returned to GBRf it was reclassified Class 66/7 and renumbered 66744. Still retaining Colas Rail Freight livery, 66744 passes on 6 August 2011 while working a Chirk–Ribblehead timber service.

Below Left – Image 120: DB Schenker (ex EWSR) Class 66/0 66048, bearing Stobart Rail livery, transfers to Toton on 13 April 2010 via a Mossend–Hams service hauled by DB Schenker (ex EWSR) Class 92 92037 *Sullivan*. 66048 had derailed at Carrbridge on 4 January 2010 on the first night of DB Schenker's operation of the Inverness–Mossend TescoLiner contract which resulted in the withdrawal of the locomotive from service and its staged move to Toton for subsequent disposal.

Below Right – Image 121: DRS Class 66/4 66434 bears Fastline livery, from its terminated lease, as it passes on 17 June 2010 while on hire to Colas Rail Freight to work its Chirk–Carlisle timber service.

Scenes from locations within the Preston area:

Top – Image 122: DB Schenker (ex EWSR) Class 66/0 66137 eases out of Preston Dock Interchange Siding on 4 July 2012 while working a Preston Dock–Lindsey Oil Refinery petroleum service.

Below – Image 123: DRS (ex Fastline) Class 66/3 66301 enters Preston on 23 November 2016 while working the Hellifield–Preston leg of a Rail Head Treatment Train (RHTT) service in top 'n' tail mode with DRS Class 66/4 66427.

Image 124: Colas Rail Freight Class 66/8 66849 *Wylam Dilly* (originally delivered to Freightliner as Class 66/5 66576) eases through Preston in the early hours of 1 April 2015 while working a Chirk–Carlisle timber service.

Image 125: The *'Royal Scotsman'* is a luxury train service that normally operates tours within Scotland but each year its tour programme includes a Tour of Britain. The tour train passed Euxton on 7 July 2019 while working the Dundee–Chester leg of the tour when it was headed by GBRf Class 66/7 66746 working in top 'n' tail mode with GBRf Class 66/7 66743 – both bearing the dedicated *'Royal Scotsman'* livery.

66746 was originally delivered to DRS as Class 66/4 66410 then re-leased to Advenza Freight to become Class 66/8 66845. When Advenza Freight ceased trading, 66845 was re-leased to GBRf but sub-leased to Colas Rail Freight while 66743 was originally delivered to DRS as Class 66/4 66407 then re-leased to Advenza Freight to become Class 66/8 66842. When Advenza Freight ceased trading, 66842 was re-leased to GBRf but sub-leased to Colas Rail Freight. When the sub-leases were terminated both locomotives were reclassified Class 66/7 and gained their current numbers.

Image 126: DRS Class 66/4 66432 + 66423 drift through Balshaw Lane Junction on 8 July 2016 while working a Crewe–Sellafield flask service.

Top Left – Image 127: GBRf Class 66/7 66718 *Gwyneth Dunwoody* bears Metronet branding as it approaches Leyland on 27 March 2013 while working a Fiddlers Ferry Power Station–Newbiggin gypsum service.

Below Left – Image 128: DRS Class 66/4 66421 + DRS (ex Fastline) Class 66/3 66305 power through Balshaw Lane Junction on 7 August 2014 while working a Carlisle–Basford Hall infrastructure service.

Below Right – Image 129: DB Schenker (ex EWSR) Class 66/0 66082 diverges onto the 'slow' line at Balshaw Lane Junction on 15 March 20214 while working an Avonmouth–Clitheroe cement service.

Image 130: DRS Class 66/4 66407 approaches Leyland on 19 December 2007 while working a Daventry–Grangemouth TescoLiner service.

Image 131: **DRS Class 66/4 66428 eases onto the Preston–Blackburn line at Lostock Hall on 3 November 2017 while working a Mountsorrel–Carlisle Civil Engineer's service.**

Image 132: **DB Schenker (ex EWSR) Class 66/0 66020 breasts Hoghton Summit on 8 August 2012 while working a Preston Docks–Lindsey Oil Refinery petroleum service.**

Image 133: The signalman at Rainford collects the single line token from the driver of EWSR Class 66/0 66060 on 23 April 2003 as the Knowsley–Immingham paper service prepares to resume its journey.

Image 134: EWSR Class 66/0 66119 rumbles past the site of the future Buckshaw Parkway station on 23 April 2003 while working a Crewe–Carlisle mgr service diverted from its normal WCML route by engineering work.

Image 135: Freightliner Class 66/5 66508 curves away from the WCML at Euxton Junction on 6 March 2005 while working a Golborne–Basford Hall spoil train diverted via Bolton due to WCML engineering works between Crewe and Preston.

Image 136: DRS Class 66/4 66424 + 66429 pass Buckshaw Parkway on 16 July 2013 while working the daily Daventry–Mossend TescoLiner, diverted from its normal WCML route by engineering work.

Image 137: Colas Rail Freight Class 66/8 66849 *Wylam Dilly* (originally delivered to Freightliner as Class 66/5 66576) curves away from the WCML at Euxton Junction on 18 July 2013 while working a Carlisle–Chirk timber service, diverted from its normal WCML route by engineering work.

Scenes at Winwick:

Left – Image 138: GBRf Class 66/7 66752 *The Hoosier State* passes on 14 July 2015 while working an Ironbridge Power Station–Liverpool Bulk Terminal mgr service.

Below – Image 139: DB Schenker (ex EWSR) Class 66/0 66013 has sister locomotives 66176 + 66101 in its consist as it curves past on 19 September 2011 while working a Carlisle–Basford Hall Civil Engineer's service.

Image 140: DRS (ex Fastline) Class 66/3 66303 + Class 66/4 66427 curve past Winwick on 13 December 2012 while working a Mossend–Daventry container service.

Image 141: DRS Class 66/4 66434, bearing Malcolm company livery, passes on 14 March 2012 while working a Daventry–Coatbridge container service.

Scenes from Liverpool/Bootle Docks:

Image 142: DB Schenker (ex EWSR) Class 66/0 66192 curves past Alexandra Dock on 24 March 2010 while working a Gladstone Dock–Arpley steel service.

Image 143: Fastline Class 66/3 66304 curves past Alexandra Dock on 19 November 2008 while working a Liverpool Bulk Terminal–Ratcliffe Power Station mgr service.

Image 144: EWSR Class 66/0 66177 curves onto Bootle Regent Road on 5 March 2003 while working a Liverpool Bulk Terminal–Pennyfford coal service.

Top Left – Image 145: Fastline Class 66/3 66305 reverses its trainset under the loader at the bulk terminal on 24 November 2008 before working forward as a Liverpool Bulk Terminal–Ratcliffe Power Station mgr service.

Below Left – Image 146: Freightliner Class 66/5 66566 curves past Alexandra Dock on 18 February 2012 having collected Freightliner Class 70 70019 + 70020 from Seaforth Dock for transit to Crewe with Freightliner Class 66/5 66954 providing rear end braking assistance.

Below Right – Image 147: Freightliner Class 66/5 66502 *Basford Hall Centenary 2001* stands in Seaforth Container Terminal on 23 May 2002 as its container trainset for Crewe is checked prior to departure.

Image 148: EWSR Class 66/0 66112 shunts the sidings of a local scrap merchant based in Gladstone Dock on 24 November 2008.

Scenes from Warrington:

Image 149: DB Schenker (ex EWSR) Class 66/0 66075 approaches Arpley yard on 24 October 2012 after reversal at Latchford Siding while working a Fiddlers Ferry Power Station–Arpley mgr service.

Image 150: DRS (ex Fastline) Class 66/3 66304 powers through Warrington Bank Quay on 6 May 2011 while working a Daventry–Coatbridge container service.

Left – Image 151: Freightliner Class 66/5 66546 curves under Warrington Bank Quay on 6 May 2011 while working a Daw Mill Colliery–Fiddlers Ferry Power Station mgr service.

Below – Image 152: GBRF Class 66/7 66735 (originally delivered to DRS as Class 66/4 66403) retains the livery of its original operator as it curves past Crosfield Level Crossing on 26 July 2011 while working a Fiddlers Ferry Power Station–Newbiggin gypsum service.

Scenes from Acton Bridge:

Top – Image 153: DB Schenker (ex EWSR) Class 66/0 66017 passes on 29 July 2015 while working a Halewood–Southampton Docks automotive service.

Below Left – Image 154: Freightliner Class 66/6 66615 passes on 12 May 2005 while working a Garston–Gresty Lane automotive service.

Below Right – Image 155: EWSR Class 66/0 66157 curves through on 12 May 2005 while working a Runcorn–Arpley chemical service.

Scenes from Peak Forest:

Left – Image 156: DB Schenker (ex EWSR) Class 66/0 66097 sets up an aggregates train for Peterborough on 26 February 2011.

Below – Image 157: DB Schenker (ex EWSR) Class 66/0 66213 passes on 26 February 2011 while working a Peak Forest–Northenden aggregates service.

Top – Image 158: DRS Class 66/4 66431 approaches on 26 February 2011 while working a Stourton–Peak Forest aggregates service.

Right – Image 159: Freightliner Class 66/5 66581 *Sophie* approaches Edale on 4 March 2008 while working a Drax Power Station–Tunstead limestone service.

Below – Image 160: GBRf Class 66/7 66785 (originally delivered to EWSR as Class 66/0 66185) sets back its Bletchley–Peak Forest trainset into CEMEX yard on 28 September 2018 for reloading with aggregates.

Engineering trains around Southport:

Image 161: EWSR Class 66/0 66190 stands at Formby on 19 February 2002 while awaiting entry to the works site with fresh ballast.

Image 162: EWSR Class 66/0 66033 stands at Hightown on 14 February 2002 while awaiting entry to the works site with fresh ballast.

Image 163: Freightliner Class 66/5 66510, working in top 'n' tail mode with Freightliner Class 70 70005, awaits departure on 19 November 2013 after reversal of its Basford Hall–Parbold engineering train.

Image 164: Freightliner Class 66/5 66511 arrives in Southport on 20 November 2013, working in top 'n' tail mode with Freightliner Class 70 70003, while working a Basford Hall–Parbold service that would be taken forward by 70003.

Image 165: Freightliner Class 66/6 66605 stands in Birkdale on 29 March 2006 with a ballast train for the engineering site.

Image 166: DB Schenker (ex EWSR) Class 66/0 66187 approaches Manchester Oxford Road on 21 November 2012 while working a Trafford Park–Southampton Docks container service.

Right – Image 167: GBRf Class 66/7 66720 provides insurance to GBRf Class 92 92014 on 8 June 2016 while the latter was under test on the Garston–Dagenham automotive service after its refurbishment following a lengthy period of storage.

Below – Image 168: A visit to Crewe Basford Hall yard on 24 June 2006 sees Freightliner's Class 66/6 66620, Class 66/5 66520, Class 66/4 (ex DRS) 66418 and Class 66/5 66526 *Driver Steve Dunn (George)* stabled awaiting their next duties.

Image 169: The preserved East Lancashire Railway (ELR) heritage line includes Freightliner employees amongst its volunteers hence its ability to obtain locomotives for Gala events as on 7 July 2002 when Freightliner Class 66/5 66508, working in top 'n' tail mode with Freightliner Class 47/0 47289, approached Ramsbottom with the 14:15 Irwell Vale–Bury service during the ELR's Annual Diesel Gala.

2.6: Wales and Borders

This region encompasses routes within the area bounded to the west by the Chester–Shrewsbury–Newport line (The Marches Line).

Image 170: Freightliner Class 66/6 66605 crosses Frodsham Viaduct on 24 March 2010 while working an Ellesmere Port–Fiddlers Ferry Power Station mgr service.

Top Right – Image 171: EWSR Class 66/0 66124 drifts past Coedkernow on 6 July 2005 while working a Corby–Margam steel service.

Below Left – Image 172: EWSR Class 66/0 66172 curves through Taffs Well on 27 February 2004 while working a Tower Colliery–Margam mgr service.

Below Right – Image 173: EWSR Class 66/0 66045 eases through Barry on 7 July 2005 while working an Aberthaw Power Station–Newport Dock mgr service.

Image 174: EWSR Class 66/0 66201 stands in Aberthaw yard on 27 February 2004 while preparing to reverse its mgr trainset into Aberthaw Power Station.

Image 175: EWSR Class 66/0 66035, working in top 'n' tail mode with EWSR Class 47/7 47737 *Resurgent*, curves through Old Colwyn on 11 June 2002 while working a return VSOE charter from Blaenau Ffestiniog to Chester.

Right – Image 176: EWSR Class 66/0 66036 curves into Aberthaw yard on 4 July 2005 while working an Avonmouth–Aberthaw Power Station mgr service.

Below – Image 177: EWSR Class 66/0 66037 curves out of Newport on 4 September 2004 while working an East Usk–Gloucester Civil Engineer's service.

2.7: Thames and Cotswolds

This region includes routes encompassed by the Birmingham–Gloucester–Bristol line to the west, the Bristol–Paddington line to the south and Paddington–Birmingham (ex GWR route) to the east.

Image 178: DB Schenker (ex EWSR) Class 66/0 66020 curves into Reading on 18 April 2011 while working a Whatley–St Pancras aggregates service.

Image 179: Freightliner Class 66/5 66577 races through the Thames Valley at Cholsey on 8 October 2004 while working a Southampton Maritime–Coatbridge container service.

Top – Image 180: Freightliner Class 66/5 66503 *The Railway Magazine* approaches Reading on 18 April 2011 while working a Bristol–Tilbury container service.

Below Left – Image 181: EWSR Class 66/0 66078 curves through Islip on 24 November 2004 while working a Didcot–Bicester MoD service.

Below Right – Image 182: EWSR Class 66/0 66176 passes Ealing Broadway on 21 October 2004 while working a Colnbrook–Chatham steel service.

Right – Image 183: Freightliner Class 66/5 66571 curves through Reading West on 22 October 2004 while working a Southampton Maritime–Trafford Park container service.

Below Left – Image 184: EWSR Class 66/0 66126 eases into Oxford on 23 September 2004 while working a Didcot–Bicester MoD service.

Below Right – Image 185: EWSR Class 66/0 66210 calls at West Drayton on 20 October 2004 while working a Chatham–Colnbrook steel service.

Left – Image 186: EWSR Class 66/0 66071 awaits departure from Banbury on 22 September 2004 while working a Ditton–Southampton Docks container service.

Above – Image 187: DB Schenker (ex EWSR) Class 66/0 66198 descends into Kings Sutton on 11 March 2011 while working a Stud Farm–Hinksey Civil Engineer's service.

Below – Image 188: Freightliner Class 66/5 66503 *The Railway Magazine* approaches Aynho North on 23 September 2004 while working a Trafford Park–Southampton Maritime container service.

Top Right – Image 189: DB Schenker (ex EWSR) Class 66/0 66102 weaves through Kings Sutton on 14 May 2014 while working a Southampton Docks–Castle Bromwich automotive service.

Below Left – Image 190: DRS Class 66/4 66422 is on hire to Freightliner on 11 March 2011 as it weaves through Kings Sutton while working a Southampton Maritime–Trafford Park container service.

Below Right – Image 191: GBRf Class 66/7 66723 *Chinook* weaves through Kings Sutton on 22 June 2016 while working an Eastleigh–Mountsorrel Civil Engineer's service.

Top Left – Image 192: DB Schenker (ex EWSR) Class 66/0 66129 weaves through Kings Sutton on 11 March 2011 while working a Theale–Lindsey Oil Refinery petroleum service.

Below Left – Image 193: Freightliner Class 66/5 66518 curves through Tyseley on 8 March 2005 while working a Hinksey–Stud Farm Civil Engineer's service.

Below Right – Image 194: Freightliner Class 66/6 66614 eases through Small Heath on 9 October 2012 while working a Westbury–Stud Farm Civil Engineer's service comprising a High Output Ballast Cleaning (HOBC) trainset.

2.8: Wessex and West Country

This region encompasses routes south of the line from Paddington to Bristol via the Berks & Hants line and west of a line from Woking to Portsmouth.

Image 195: EWSR Class 66/ 66209 curves off the Tamar Bridge on 20 July 2005 while working a Burngullow–Irvine china clay service.

Top Left – Image 196: EWSR Class 66/0 66010 passes Little Bedwyn on 2 March 2004 while working a Westbury–Hayes aggregates service.

Below Left – Image 197: Freightliner Class 66/5 66580 is devoid of branding as it passes Basingstoke on 18 April 2011 while en route from Eastleigh to Hoo Junction where it will join the GBRf fleet to become Class 66/7 66740.

Below Right – Image 198: Freightliner Class 66/5 66554 approaches Basingstoke on 18 April 2011 while working a Southampton Maritime–(Birmingham) Lawley St container service.

Image 199: DB Schenker (ex EWSR) Class 66/0 66149 weaves through Basingstoke on 18 April 2011 while working a Halewood–Southampton Docks automotive service.

Scenes from Eastleigh during a visit on 3 July 2014:

Image 200: GBRF Class 66/7 66740 (originally delivered to Freightliner as Class 66/5 66580) curves through while working a Mountfield–Southampton Docks gypsum service.

Image 201: DB Schenker (ex EWSR) Class 66/0 66095 approaches while working a Southampton Docks–Eastleigh automotive service.

Image 202: **DB Schenker (ex EWSR) Class 66/0 66008 approaches while working a Southampton Docks–Eastleigh automotive service.**

Image 203: DB Schenker (ex EWSR) Class 66/0 66201 + 66105 depart with an Eastleigh–Westbury Civil Engineer's service.

Image 204: GBRf Class 66/7 66713 *Forest City* stands in Eastleigh Works yard after being repainted in the latest corporate livery.

Left – Image 205: EWSR Class 66/0 66060 approaches Bathampton Junction on 26 November 2004 while working a Didcot–Westbury coal service.

Below – Image 206: EWSR Class 66/0 66078 approaches Fairwood Junction on 8 June 2004 while working a Purley–Merehead aggregates service.

Image 207: GBRf Class 66/7 66718 *Sir Peter Hendry CBE* approaches Fairwood Junction on 17 March 2014 while working a Wellingborough–Whatley aggregates service.

Left – Image 208: Freightliner Class 66/6 66601 *The Hope Valley* reverses its trainset through Coombe en route to Moorswater yard on 30 November 2004 while working an Earles Sidings–Moorswater cement service.

Below – Image 209: EWSR Class 66/0 66202 leads a sister Class 66/0 locomotive as they ascend Rattery Bank on 27 November 2004 while working an Exeter–Tavistock Junction Civil Engineer's service.

2.9: South and South East

This region encompasses routes east of the line from Reading to Havant, south of the Waterloo–Reading line and all lines in Kent and Sussex.

Image 210: Colas Rail Freight Class 66/8 66845 (originally delivered to DRS as Class 66/4 66410) bears the livery of its previous operator as it drifts through Kensington Olympia on 26 August 2010 while working a Dollands Moor–Hams Hall container service.

Image 211: GBRf Class 66/7 66778 *Darius Cheskin* enters Lewisham on 29 August 2019 while working an Eastleigh–Hoo Junction Civil Engineer's service.

Image 212: EWSR Class 66/0 66007 approaches Wandsworth Road on 2 September 2005 while working a Wembley–Thamesport container service.

Image 213: DB Cargo (ex EWSR) Class 66/0 66155 passes Wandsworth Road on 30 August 2019 as it heads for Stewarts Lane with an aggregates service from Cliffe Brett Marine.

Image 214: DB Cargo (ex EWSR) Class 66/0 66126 curves into Wandsworth Road on 30 August 2019 while working a Churchyard Sidings–Hither Green aggregates service.

Image 215: Freightliner Class 66/5 66558 forms part of the consist on 29 August 2019 when the Hoo Junction–Eastleigh Civil Engineer's service was noted passing Crayford hauled by GBRf Class 66778 *Darius Cheskin*.

Image 216: Colas Rail Freight Class 66/8 66849 *Wylam Dilly* (originally delivered to Freightliner as Class 66/5 66576) drifts through Lewisham on 29 August 2019 while engaged in route learning duties between Hoo Junction and Colnbrook.

Image 217: Freightliner Class 66/6 66602 eases through Hither Green on 30 August 2019 while working a Whatley Quarry–Hothfield aggregates service; this was one of the haulage contracts recently gained by Freightliner to haul Mendips aggregates traffic.

Image 218: Freightliner Class 66/6 66618 *Railways Illustrated Annual Photographic Awards – Alan Barnes* curves through Hither Green on 30 August 2019 while working a Colnbrook BAA–Grain Oil Terminal fuel service.

Image 219: Freightliner Class 66/6 66622 powers through Crayford on 29 August 2019 while working a Grain Oil Terminal–Colnbrook BAA fuel service.

Image 220: GBRf Class 66/7 66780 *The Cemex Express* (originally delivered to EWSR as Class 66/0 66008) bears Cemex company livery as it drifts through Petts Wood on 30 August 2019 while working a Crawley–Tonbridge aggregates service.

2.10: Scotland

This region encompasses routes north of the line from Gretna to Berwick on Tweed.

Image 221: DB Schenker (ex EWSR) Class 66/0 66163 passes Saughton on 3 May 2008 while working a Mossend–Millerhill infrastructure service.

Image 222: EWSR Class 66/0 66249 nears the summit of Beattock on 4 March 2004 while working an Ayr–Fiddlers Ferry Power Station mgr service.

Scenes from Dinwoodie, north of Lockerbie:

Image 223: DRS Class 66/4 66423 heads north on 19 April 2013 while working a Daventry–Coatbridge container service.

Image 224: Freightliner Class 66/5 66585 *The Drax Flyer* + 66554 head south on 15 June 2013 while working a Killoch Colliery–Leeds Stourton mgr service.

Image 225: DRS Class 66/4 66431 + 66426 head north on 13 May 2016 while working a Daventry–Mossend TescoLiner service.

Image 226: EWSR Class 66/0 66191 eases into Berwick-upon-Tweed on 16 June 2005 while working an Ayr–Ratcliffe Power Station mgr service

Image 227: **EWSR Class 66/0 66112 crosses the Forth Bridge on 9 March 2004 while working a Hartlepool–Inverness pipe service.**

Image 228: EWSR Class 66/0 66194 crosses the Forth Bridge on 16 August 2007 while working a Longannet Power Station–Hunterston mgr service.

Right – Image 229: EWSR Class 66/0 66149 crosses the Forth Bridge on 12 February 2003 while working a Millerhill–Longannet Power Station mgr service.

Below – Image 230: GBRf Class 66/7 66746 bears dedicated *'Royal Scotsman'* livery as it crosses the Forth Bridge on 20 July 2019 while working the Dundee–Edinburgh leg of a *'Royal Scotsman'* railtour. 66746 was delivered to DRS as Class 66/4 66410 then re-leased to GB Railfreight but sub-leased to Colas Rail Freight where it became Class 66/8 66845. When returned to GB Railfreight it was reclassified Class 66/7 and renumbered 66746.

Image 231: An unidentified Freightliner Class 66/6 locomotive approaches Dalmeny on 25 April 2011 while working an Aberdeen–Oxwellmains cement service.

Right – Image 232: EWSR Class 66/0 66035 curves past Spittal on 9 November 2004 while working a Tyne Yard–Millerhill mgr service.

Below – Image 233: EWSR Class 66/0 66119 passes Saughton on 11 February 2003 while working a Longannet Power Station–Millerhill mgr service.

Image 234: EWSR Class 66/0 66077 *Benjamin Gimbert GC* is pilotted by EWSR Class 66/0 66236 as they pass Whitemoss on 26 May 2005 while working an Aberdeen–Mossend 'Enterprise' service.

Top Right – Image 235: EWSR Class 66/0 66108 pilots Class 67 67008 past Forteviot on 26 May 2005 while working an Inverness–Mossend 'Enterprise' service.

Below Left – Image 236: EWSR Class 66/0 66077 *Benjamin Gimbert GC* passes along the Forth foreshore at Culross on 6 April 2005 while working a Longannet Power Station–Hunterston mgr service.

Below Right – Image 237: EWSR Class 66/0 66242 passes along the Forth foreshore at Culross on 6 April 2005 while working a Hunterston–Longannet Power Station mgr service.

Image 238: **EWSR Class 66/0 66113 pilots EWSR Class 67 67008 past Bannockburn on 5 April 2005 while working an Inverness–Mossend 'Enterprise' service.**

Image 239: EWSR Class 66/0 66232 slows to a halt in Dunkeld on 24 May 2004 while working a Millerhill–Pitlochry Civil Engineer's ballast service.

Image 240: EWSR Class 66/0 66110 pilots EWSR Class 67 67004 through Pitlochry on 25 May 2005 while working an Inverness–Mossend 'Enterprise' service.

Top Right – Image 241: EWSR Class 66/0 66186 crosses Stonehaven Viaduct on 8 March 2004 while working an Aberdeen–Laurencekirk pipe service having …

Below Left – Image 242: … spent the previous day stabled in Aberdeen Guild St.

Below Right – Image 243: DRS Class 66/4 66404 speeds through Blackford on 16 June 2004 while working a Grangemouth–Aberdeen TescoLiner service.

Image 244: GBRf Class 66/7 66737 *Lesia* (originally delivered to DRS as Class 66/4 66405) pilots GBRf Class 73/9 73969 on 22 July 2016 as they await departure from Edinburgh Waverley while working the Inverness portion of the northbound 'Highlander' sleeper service.

Top Right – Image 245: GBRf Class 66/7 66705 *Golden Jubilee* pilots GBRf Class 73/9 73967 as they arrive in Edinburgh Waverley in the early hours of 22 July 2016 while working the Aberdeen portion of the southbound 'Highlander' sleeper service.

Below Left – Image 246: Freightliner Class 66/6 66609 eases through Edinburgh's Princes St Gardens on 10 November 2004 while working an Oxwellmains–Viewpark cement service.

Below Right – Image 247: Freightliner Class 66/6 66610 curves into Pitlochry on 31 August 2006 while working an Inverness–Oxwellmains cement service.

Image 248: EWSR Class 66/0 66051 passes Falkirk Grahamston on 4 March 2004 while working a Mossend–Grangemouth container service.

Image 249: GBRf Class 66/7 66743 carries dedicated *'Royal Scotsman'* livery as it crosses Jamestown Viaduct on 25 May 2018 while working the Dundee–Edinburgh leg of a *'Royal Scotsman'* Tour. 66743 was originally delivered to DRS as Class 66/4 66407 then re-leased to Advenza Freight to become Class 66/8 66842. When Advenza Railfreight ceased trading, 66842 was re-leased by GBRf sub-leased to Colas Rail Freight but when returned to GB Railfreight it was reclassified Class 66/7 and renumbered 66743.

Image 250: EWSR Class 66/0 66112 runs over the Horseshoe Curve on 18 June 2005 while working the Fort William–Mossend 'Enterprise' service which had no traffic on this day.

Section 3:
Finale

In 2016 the Class 66 production ceased when new EU emission regulations came into force and GBRf took delivery of the final locomotive – Class 66/7 66779. To mark the final production the locomotive was given a lined green livery and named *Evening Star*, in a style similar to that applied to Standard Class 9 2-10-0 92220 to mark its status as the final steam locomotive to be built by a British Railways workshop.

Image 251: The pair of locomotives was displayed in the National Rail Museum at York on 10 May 2016 when 66779 was revealed to the public for the first time. (*Image courtesy of Richard Tuplin/Railway Herald*)

Image 252: Seen in normal service GBRf Class 66/7 66779 *Evening Star* approaches Newton le Willows on 1 October 2018 while working a Drax Power Station–Liverpool Bulk Terminal mgr service.